Seven Last Words

Praise for *Seven Last Words*

“It’s not what you expect: Jesus is there, but under layers of Mama and boyhood memory, discerned through a haze of cancer and longing. Terry Minchow-Proffit’s direct and simple language strikes somewhere deep in the spirit where only poetry can.”

~Steve Hollaway, poet, author, and pastor of Harbor Baptist Church, Block Island, RI

“In these seven poems, the world keeps ‘getting to us’ in small and large ways, though mostly large: the travails of terminal illness, the moral injury of the Holocaust. These wounds are always tempered by love, like Mary’s for her Son, that ‘tenders the distance down.’ In the face of circumstances that mingle the height of love and the depth of suffering and grief, the poet reconfirms his faith. Faith like that of the seminary student in Chekhov’s story ‘The Student’: that when we reimagine and emotionally connect with the past, we take an interest, with our whole being, in the souls of people we know only through stories—and, through them, our own souls. The loving care demonstrated towards others in these poems is a detailed care, set within the poet's private roles and relationships, and extending to the poet's careful yet exuberant choice of words.”

~Rebecca Starks, Editor-in-chief, *Mud Season Review*

“In his poetry, Terry Minchow-Proffitt takes a thought—an image, a phrase, a moment—and unfolds it until the reader can see the sublime that had been hidden in the creases. He employs a close, painterly attention to detail and language, and his work is truly inspired, in the full old-fashioned meaning of that word: deeply informed by tradition, yet full of a fresh breath.”

~Rosemary Zimmermann, Poetry Editor, *Friends Journal*

“This cycle of seven poems is like a crucifix made of stained glass in which the image of our own reflection overlays the image of Christ. At each moment—in a curtained space in a cancer treatment center, in fatherly motion beneath a great tree, or on the cross itself—Minchow-Proffitt renders a complete and poetically complex union between our individual longings and all longing, our sufferings and all suffering, between ours and Christ’s.”

~Chuck Hussung, poet and teacher, St. Louis University High School

“In a sense, Jesus is always living, dying, and living again. Terry Minchow-Proffitt's poems compress the energy of that then-and-there, here-and-now event into language which cannot finally hold it. His words have their feet on the ground of pain, but they head for an unrealized but real hope. When I read them, I know that, even though it's likely to take a long time, we'll get home.”

~Dr. Guy Sayles, author, former pastor of First Baptist Church of Asheville, NC and member of the religion faculty at Mars Hill University

“In his seventh poem of *Seven Last Words*, Terry Minchow-Proffitt writes, ‘We press on, less driven than drawn.’ In a phrase, this captures the compelling power of this intimate collection of poems. In an age when many in the Christian movement communicate through bombast and intimidation, Terry pierces the heart of the reader by simply and memorably connecting human travail with the death of Christ. Although that sounds like it might be depressing or oppressive, somehow, through the filter of his experience, Terry’s poems draw us closer to the great mystery and nourish us because they ring so true to life.”

~Rev. John Burns, author and pastor, University Baptist Church, College Park, MD

“Many would be converted to free verse poetry lovers if all free verse hit as hard and true as Terry Minchow-Proffitt's *Seven Last Words.* No wimpy compartmentalization is allowed in these poems; no religion on Sundays, grief during funeral week, get back to work and ‘keep your mind off of it’. This poetry shows the muscle involved in the integration of our lives and the towering humanity of those who work for personal truth. If I needed to use only one word for description, it would have to be ‘powerful’.”

~Frances McColl Stewart, poet and author

“A synthesis of ancient utterance and contemporary (yet ageless) aspects of the divine-human equation are plumbed to create the crux of this spare yet redolent volume. *Seven Last Words* seeps sumptuously into the reader’s soul, inspiring a fresh sense of spiritual awareness, viscous with the verity of connotation.”

~Gloria J. Wimberley, author and Professor of English at Eastern Gateway Community College

Seven Last Words

Terry Minchow-Proffitt

Middle Island Press

2015

Seven Last Words

All the poems in *Seven Last Words* were originally published in *Mud Season Review* (Issue #3, November 2014).

ISBN 978-0692373309

Front cover art: "When Love Is Revealed"
and back cover art: "The Village" by Emily Mitchell
Interior art by Emily Mitchell

Published by Middle Island Press
PO Box 354
West Union, WV 26456

middleislandpress.com

For Sandy, my wife, and my children, Zak and Hannah:
Your abiding love and encouragement
convince me that God, too, has a loving face.
Whatever cross I bear, you make it lighter.

Contents

ACKNOWLEDGMENTS

This chapbook of poems based on The Seven Last Words of Christ rose organically through the gracious and fertile soil of community. Where it began exactly is hard to figure, but we can trace the mystery at least as far back as two small congregations in the Arkansas delta: quiet and serious Second Baptist Church in West Helena, where I was baptized as a child, and my grandparents' toe-tapping, hand-clapping Assembly of God church in Dyess. There, in these two houses of worship, we lived in the urgent shadow of Jesus and his cross.

Later, I'm pretty sure these poems hitched a well-disguised ride as sermons preached in the congregations I pastored for 27 years: University Baptist Church, Salt Lake City, Utah; Broadneck Baptist Church in Annapolis, Maryland; Broadview Baptist Church in Temple Hills, Maryland; and, finally, Dayspring Baptist Church in Town and Country, Missouri, where they first emerged as poetry through an invitation to lead a class on Christ's Last Words during Lent of 2013. I'm indebted to, and grateful for, this class's gracious attentiveness and support.

A loyal cadre of friends welcomed each poem's slow surfacing through painstaking revision: John Burns, Scott Darwin, Alex Davis, John Harrison, Steve Hollaway, Chuck Hussung, Coles L'Hommedieu, Daye Phillippo, Drew Phillips, Guy Sayles, Douglass Sullivan-Gonzalez.

Along the way, poet Ed Mullany was kind enough to offer his generous attention. Ed's close reading and input proved both wise and encouraging.

The editors and staff at *Mud Season Review*, in particular Rebecca Starks and Rosemary Zimmerman, were the first to see, and risk, the promise of publication. Their encouraging feedback and sage suggestions helped me discover each poem anew with increased vitality and clarity. They were also the first to pair the beautiful art of Emily Mitchell with my poetry, a grace that Emily was generous enough to extend further to these pages.

Two friends and colleagues in particular, Belden Lane and Matthew Lippman, have championed my recent foray into poetry. They are my mentors and friends; they know my voice well and hold me to it.

Finally, I want to thank my editor at Middle Island Press, Christina Anne Taylor, whose careful and attentive eye assured that this little book was given its best shot at landing in *your* hands—and, I hope, your hearts—with my lasting gratitude and love.

Foreword

by

Matthew Lippman

Do you remember the controversy that came with the release of Marty Scorsese's epic picture *The Last Temptation of Christ?* All that talk about God as Man and Man as God, divinity wrapped up with humanness, and the firestorm that followed because Christ was depicted, especially in the last third of the film, as being so particularly flawed? His soul filled beautifully with longing and lust and sorrow and desire and mindfulness and love. I found it magical. As magical as Terry Minchow-Proffitt's set of poems, "Last Words," which deal with the last seven spoken signatures of Christ as he died on the cross. These are some of the most profoundly meaningful poems I have read in a long time—as a Jew, as a poet, as a citizen of the planet—because of the way in which they meet, head-on, the conflict between devotion and rebellion when it comes to Christ. They are perhaps the most spiritually based expressions of honest religiosity that I have read.

Terry is a retired pastor. But still a pastor. I have had the pleasure of reading his work for years, of being inside his poems. I feel connected to them because they are connected. To The Delta, to his children, to his God. God is with him all the time. A kind of God, I imagine, that seeps out of his eyes and pores and muscles at each crisis, or each day when feeding the chickens or walking the dog. He's a man of the cloth who has devoted his life to love, with nothing outside its scope—God, humankind, family, trees, children, language.

God is Love. God is the Word. The Word is Love.

The spirit is large here in Terry's words, as if some otherworldly but very grounded muse touched down in his heart. The paintings of Emily Mitchell capture my sense of this muse: a dragonfly seen up close and still, the graceful naked back of a woman looking out the window, full of color and piano and grace. The spirit is equal parts holy and human. Plunging us into discomfort, the poems then gently guide us back to safety, poise, and grace. He navigates the visionary with his unique, particular vision, and hears final words with a poet's ear, always attuned to the possibility of revision. The work of listening and responding is never finished. Is ever now, surprising us at every turn.

Seven
Last
Words

✣ I ✣

Father, forgive them; for they do not know what they are doing.

(Luke 23:34)

Looks like we'll spend the better part
of Valentine's Day together
at the cancer center, sitting
with our backs against the window
beneath this morning light angling down
warm across our shoulders,
our serious sighs exiled
back to our senses.

You're crunching the ice chips
while the nurse thumps your wan arm
for that one vein that doesn't roll.
In my head I'm off doing my best
math with your blood count,
while my face and mouth do their most
optimistic shtick to distract
you from coming undone:
This'll make you stronger, honey.
But you're not buying any of it—
only this held hand
up against
the infusion of iron.

The skimpy curtain they've drawn florid
around us is no wall. Strangers on both sides
suffer by a distance of inches.
No matter how hard we try to imagine ourselves *sub rosa*,
how low like a confession we keep our voices,
we can't help but eavesdrop
on one another making do:
Here's your pillow from home . . . How's that?

We suffer discreetly, relax and lie
back with our juice
before all the determined
needles and tubes, the plastic sagging
bags, and the pester of beeps
that never quit bleating about
how some fluid has gone
and clogged up, pinched to,
won't go again until
measured by the numbers, recalibrated,
set straight just so
we can resume talking and taking
into our veins the latest toxin as ransom.

If I close my eyes, I can all but see
the two of us back from the brink.
Say, at dinner,
maybe at Ruby Tuesday,

assorted sentiment in hand:
chocolates in a heart-shaped box,
a Hallmark card, a single rose, dessert for two—
there they are, and just us too,
bungling about
above all this tin-foiled red
as your color returns.

ꙮ II ꙮ

Truly, I tell you, today you will be with me in Paradise.

(Luke 23:43)

His Holiness the 14th Dalai Lama of Tibet
was quick to answer when asked,
"If you could meet Jesus, what would you like to ask him?"
He replied: "What is the nature of the Father?"

Not so fast, Your Holiness.
Ask me if I could meet Jesus, and I wouldn't
ask about the Father, wouldn't even
rag on Him like I used to.
Really. I'm done with that.
I'm down with the Father.
Am one, in fact, the hapless
grateful sort that's still married
at 57 with two kids raised.
It's the nature of the son
that gets me.

I've been missing of late
the son I was—wondering where he's gone,
how the innocent moment's solid hold

keeps dissolving like Tibet,
forgotten:

Early on, a boy,
that summer by the ditch
under the cottonwood in the front yard,
finds himself out of the blue
lifted by his own daddy's arms
into the green-diamond shade
while birdsong and breeze clatter
silver in the leaves over his head.
Is this where you first felt the rough bark?

I seek for God's sake
not what happened, or even what might happen—
I want the *happening* to happen again
back inside the moment without why
when it's not yet dawned
that there are words
to invite back Paradise,
this boy, Father-whisked
as if by whim, whorled
within the canopied tree
by the wrung, wracked middle
of his most fluent longing:
Jesus, remember me . . .

“The Shadow of My Former Self” by Emily Mitchell

ꕤ III ꕤ

Woman, behold thy son! . . . Behold thy mother!

(John 19:26-27)

When Jesus looked down and saw
Mary's face tilted up—
pale blue, disconsolate,
delicate too—
what would you guess he said?
Maybe at first he fumbled, *Your face.*
Or flinching, tried to console, *Mama,*
don't cry, don't.

Chances are, out came, *Mama,*
you cannot . . . because she could not bygod
get her hands on those in power, not get
back at the betrayers in the body
as they surely could her.
So he begged,
Don't, Mama, don't.

So she did not, but did
what she could: stared up
through the long dying
of her first vow to the Angel.

The Bible says Jesus said,
Woman, behold . . .
then stole a far cry from that stable,
family trips to the lake,
his first fish, that first dive,
always tending too far from shore,
Mary's nervous bead on his buoyant head
bobbing distant on the face of a lake
so bright and immense it hurt to look.

Whatever later was said Jesus said,
my money's on *Mama,*
behold your son: his friable body
grimed with spit and gall, still
in her eye who he was
before the world
got to him,
how he tenders the distance down
with a voice as familiar and laden as the One
her hands can no longer reach—
Son.

☙ IV ❧

My God, my God, why have you forsaken me?
(Matthew 27:46)

That miserable night in the boat,
as Lake Gennesaret pitched gray against
the Apostles, their hearts hardening with each stroke
till they slumped, huffing over the oars
in that grim blue hour before daybreak, you strolled
across the white-capped rile
with the calm nerve of a ghost, as if
you might have passed them by.

That day in Jericho, blind Bartimaeus
hunkered by the roadside in the heat
with his hand out, all but
lost in the crowd's ire
and dust. He cried
until you heeded,
but not before it seemed
the scales might never fall
from his eyes, or yours, as if
you might have passed him by.

But now you stay put,
pinned to the point of shriek, bereft.
Elijah will not come.
We wag our heads and walk on.

How our days can be long;
we are as derelict as you once were.
Nothing is as it appears.
Your cry and our cry,
my God, is always and ever only one cry, as if
from the Garden to the Tree
we are all rigged for reprieve,
calling and calling on the fly,
My God, do not pass us by.

℘ V ℘

I thirst.

(John 19:28)

Come to me, Lord, those nights
when you might find
me at a loss, sitting
close in the quiet,
at the dinner table, staring
into the next lamp-lit room
over a bowl of Frosted Mini-Wheats.

It might be the tail end of a great day.
Friends called and my stock rose.
Maybe all day long the sky was blue
and I was able to say exactly that,
with words, on paper: *The sky was blue.*
Or it could have been one of *those* days.
You know, like when your puppy mauls
the extension cord in the backyard
that snakes to your pond's pump,
which means seven goldfish might asphyxiate
by dawn, and the sorry culprit now lies at your feet,
fevered and moaning, with a mangled

lock of 16-gauge electrical cord
powering up her belly
to a gurgling pitch, all staticky,
like your first transistor radio.

You were twelve, turning the dime-sized dial
with the pure intent of a monk, the prayerful
dexterity of a thief about to crack
the safe of a lifetime, your longing
held ear-close but never quite tuned in,
The Monkees always off, garbled
between stations—maybe it was a day like that.

It doesn't really matter what kind of day it is, Lord,
when you come close and I've grown quiet
in my wanting, out of words enough now
to quaff up your silence and call it a night
with our naked thirsts intact,
as you countenance away
the whole
sacred shebang.

≈ VI ≈

It is finished.
(John 19:30)

Rabbi Herschel Schacter, a chaplain
in Patton's Third Army, rode a commandeered Jeep
through the gates of Buchenwald.

Smoke was still rising, flesh
burning, bodies strewn
everywhere still . . .

a week after Passover. It seemed all done,
as though no one was left
alive. He found himself running

wanting only
to know: "Are there any Jews alive here?"
when he came to the place, Kleine Lager,

where thin Juden were alive, lying
stacked to the ceiling on raw wooden planks.
They stared down at the rabbi, frightened

taut by his unfamiliar uniform.
He could not cry quickly enough,
Shalom Aleichem, Yidden, ihr zint frei!

II

Jesus, in your livid love,
with eyes that see some semblance
of victory, you cry, "It is finished!"

We hear your cry but
can't quite make it out:
Yiddish? Latin? One word in Greek?

Something foreign rooted
as all words in all languages:
Consummatum est.

The one word that death
cannot bear and fear
cannot shake: Consummation

rides through our forced gates,
allied suffering runs
at this late hour

breathless, barracks to barracks,
as if obtained from air: "Peace be upon you,
it is finished!"

III

Jesus, at this ninth hour—
thrashed, jabbed, racked—
you appear to be done.

But even now you look long,
as though through
your yellowing

body you hold all
horror as the charred brunt
of wrecked hope.

You are a new kind of enemy.
Your suffering
suffuses.

Our final undoing
you are, as we are
yours.

*Inspired by an obituary by Margalit Fox in *The New York Times* (3/26/13).

"Roots" by Emily Mitchell

℘ VII ℘

Father, into your hands I commend my spirit.

(Luke 23:46)

H*ere*, Lord, fixed on *this* Friday of our oily unction,
where the clouds never part
but settle in low over this copse of crosses,
we breathe in wet cement:
Our lungs harden like two small fists.

Here the mercy you threatened us with
ends up in the thick of it, down where embers still
what only you and maybe a terminally-ill cancer patient
can see: how the chest wall, stricken,
winces to nothing and outs
the blue-red cavity, the rib-barred hold
in the middle where something liver-colored
glistens and thumps.

And everybody's got one, a heart, you see.
Try it—your ass-buster boss taking a long lunch,
Commie Democrats, Republicans even, blow-hard
preachers yipping red-faced about jeezus.

Everywhere hearts.
It's how we get home, even now, maybe
without a dime to our name in this land of want,
or without a word in our mouth for what
we might say for ourselves once we're found out.
We press on, less driven than drawn
by the trust that maybe, Lord, you only see hearts.

But how can I abandon myself to you, Lord, except
while hurling my defiant cry at your absence,
how it is
to pray and pray
while Nick's cancer splits his throat
in three places and sprouts through the wounds.
Whatever's next, this happened.

I hold you to your word, just as you held the Father to his,
not knowing to this day whose hands these are,
or even who prays these words:
I come to the end,
and you are still with me.

Afterword

by

Belden Lane

"I got to keep movin.' I got to keep movin.' Blues fallin' down like hail. There's a hellhound on my trail." These words might have been spoken from the cross, given an Arkansas Delta idiom. Instead they were sung by a rambling bluesman named Robert Johnson in 1937. King of the Delta Blues Singers and best known for his song "Hell Hound on My Trail," he'd been pursued throughout his life by the devil—or was it God? For all we know, he might well have read Francis Thompson's "The Hound of Heaven."

Terry Minchow-Proffitt wrestles with the same demons that plagued (and blessed) these two earlier minstrels of the road. His poetry is shaped by the distinctive sense of place and musical rhythms of the Arkansas Delta, the soul of the South. It's an area formed by a series of tributaries that flow into the Mississippi along the eastern edge of the state: the St. Francis, the White, and the Arkansas. The land's history is filled with cotton and soybean fields, the memory of sharecroppers, racial injustice, Pentecostal religion, and of course music—blues, gospel, country, R & B. Terry himself grew up in West Helena and the little town of Dyess, the boyhood home of Johnny Cash.

Poets (and song-writers) create out of the landscapes that form them. This is what fascinates me about Terry's work. It's not as obvious in this particular cycle of poems, but it's there. It's a poetry that rings with the cadence of a Mississippi County storyteller sitting on an over-turned bucket under a shade tree. You see it in some of his earlier poems like "Helena Bound" where "a plywood sheet / nailed across the storefront window/ on Cherry Street is not the saddest thing / I ever saw, but for the 1000th time / I forget what is." Or "Secondhand Smoke" in which a child vacantly "watches the penny / taped to the needle that spins / Nat King Cole's "Stardust" / from the veneered Zenith."[1] This is more than a poetry of nostalgia. It touches the visceral core of the human soul.

How do you retrieve the raw passion and soulful agony of the last words of Christ on the cross? That's what Terry asks himself in the poems in this book. It isn't easy. For centuries they've been wrapped in a shroud of great art, classical music, and Good Friday sermons galore. How do we hear them anew against the backdrop of paint peeling off the wall of the waiting room at Crittenden Regional Hospital in West Memphis? Or the smell of beer and cigarette smoke in one of the juke joints on Biscuit Row in Helena? Or the collapsing porch of an old frame house down the road from the E-Z Mart in Turkey Scratch? What this book does is to give us first-century Jerusalem made real in the sounds and smells and lost dreams of eastern Arkansas.

Here we see a flesh and blood Mary standing at the foot of the cross, wishing she could "bygod get her hands on those in power." Her son has to say, "Don't, Mama, don't." Here we find a bedraggled nurse brushing aside needles and tubes, thumping the wan arm of a patient, looking for a "vein that doesn't roll," delivering a toxin that isn't able to heal. Here we see a small boy lifted in his daddy's arms under a cottonwood tree, remembering that summer day years later and wanting its "*happening* to happen again." Daring to imagine the impossible possibility of spending "this day" in paradise.

I know and love this man, Terry Minchow-Proffitt. We've met every month for years, reading our work to each other over coffee. Offering encouragement. Responding to what we see to be honest in each other's writing. He's a man who raises chickens, quotes Carl Jung, loves country music, preaches without notes, and reads the great poets. I've driven with him through the Arkansas Ozarks, passing dying communities and hardscrabble farms. We've walked through the broken remains of Dogpatch USA, a defunct theme park in Newton County that once celebrated the area's hillbilly image. We've floated the Buffalo National River, looking for caves and waterfalls that could take us back to a time before failed economies, before Arkansas turned into artificial images of itself, before songs were filled with nothing but the blues. We found ourselves with alt-country singer-songwriter Jim White, "looking for the gold tooth in God's crooked smile."

We could see the glint of gold, but there's always been the pain. Christ has always been dying on the cross and uttering last words... in every culture, every place. The need each time is to make it real. Local, specific, vernacular. The blues have ever been "a low-down achin' heart disease," Robert Johnson wrote in another of his songs. There *is* no generic language for grief, anger, or hope. That's what is so refreshing about this collection of poems. It takes us back to the cross...right there in the Arkansas Delta. In the heart of

Phillips County, for example. September, 1919. The Elaine race riot. Black sharecroppers shot and hanged. Blood running. Mothers in anguish. Words muttered yet again, "My God, my God, why have you forsaken me?" Again.

Can we listen? Can we see it now? Only when we *do*—only when we attend with the punctured senses of the heart—can we glimpse the visitation of a purple dragonfly on a green field. Witness love revealed in exploding color on a summer canvas. See dimly beyond the cross to a world of possibility uncovered by Emily Mitchell's brush. Only then is our suspicion of resurrection confirmed.

---

[1] See Terry Minchow-Proffitt, "Helena Bound," *Deep South Magazine* (April, 2013) and "Secondhand Smoke," *Oxford American* (Fall Issue, 2010).

"The Visitation" by Emily Mitchell

Interview

with
Mud Season Review

What inspired you to write this set of poems? Did you begin with The Seven Last Words, or did one of these poems lead you to them as a way of structuring your thoughts and experiences?

I've long been drawn in by The Seven Last Words. I was a Baptist pastor for 27 years. Being more liturgical Baptists, we'd revisit those words each year, either throughout Lent or during the Good Friday Tenebrae Service. After I retired, I was invited to teach a class on the Last Words during Lent 2013. I decided, as my personal discipline, to try to write a poem a week on each Word. I'm a slow writer, so I was well into the season of Easter before I'd finished the cycle. After letting them sit for awhile, I returned to rework them intermittently. The most recent and final revision occurred when your editors at *Mud Season* offered to workshop them with me. So here they are.

Inspiration is a big mystery to me, but there's something real about the cross that cuts to the chase and draws me in. I'm not referring to elaborate atonement theories, though there's some very exciting atonement theology happening these days, much of it prompted by the insights into mimetic violence by René Girard. But what strikes me most is the notion that God is willing to become the crucified instead of the crucifier, the notion that that reality is best known as Suffering Love. As a Christian, I believe we're called both to receive and embody such poignant love as passionately as we can. I'm drawn in by the experiential aspect of this notion.

Your question ties together two poles of how inspiration might work for me. In these poems I began with The Seven Last Words because they seemed to promise a way of structuring and deepening my sense of God's presence when life turns particularly dark and meaningless. Laurence Freeman once put it this way, speaking of Jesus: "His continuing presence within the absence created by his death is the gospel's essential message." That about says it.

You're a retired pastor. In this set of poems the connection between your faith and your poetry is explicit, but do you see a deeper connection between the two? Do you think you approach poetry differently because of your faith?

Yes and no. Integration and wholeness (integrity) matter a lot to me, so I hope that there's an abiding connection between the poems I write and my faith. While I believe faith informs my writing, I also hold that all persons have some type of faith, some notion that they trust for their life's sake, whether explicitly religious or not, and that such trust distinguishes them in their journey. Theologian Paul Tillich spoke of this as an "ultimate concern" in his classic *Dynamics of Faith*.

So I believe all poets approach their writing uniquely, based on how transformed they are by what they trust to be most true, good and beautiful. For example, I don't believe that Mark Strand claims to be particularly religious, certainly not Christian. But his "Poem After the Seven Last Words" in *Man and Camel* is a stunning witness to faith. He might not say that poetry is prayer, as I would, but when I read these I feel as though I've entered prayer.

The Seven Last Words are the seven phrases the Bible records Jesus as saying on the cross. Exploring these phrases in these poems, how did you navigate the weight of church traditions that have been laid on them over the years?

Of all the disciples, Thomas is the one I feel closest to. I'm a transplant to Missouri and have adopted the "Show Me" motto. I resonate with Thomas' refusal to take another person's word for what matters most, to want to see and feel it firsthand. And yet, when the risen Jesus comes to him in the upper room, we're never told that he follows through on Jesus' invitation to trace his wounds with his fingers. I like to think that, once in Jesus' presence, Thomas dropped his demands. In fact, the real blessing, John's Gospel says, comes to those how have not seen but believed. I count myself among these blessed souls who have never had the chance to meet Jesus in the flesh. I have come to faith largely through the faithful witness of others. I listen to their stories and learn, seeking to sift out what my mind and heart can abide as real.

All the gospels have been edited and revised by primitive Christian communities and other unknown, unnamed scribes along the way. So The Seven Last Words, though in the classic sense continuing to speak across the ages, weren't necessarily *last*. Scripture is not journalism, but communal, embodied *witness*, words arising out of the risk of a lived faith. This captivates me. I love that these words have the early church's fingerprints all over them. Such accretions and redactions are in keeping with my thoroughly incarnational sense of God. I'm called to be both discerning yet open with my faith. By the way, it also reaffirms for me that writing is indeed revision!

Could you talk to us about the inspiration for poem VI in particular? Did you worry that it might be controversial to bring together Christianity and the Holocaust in the way you do here?

The experience of writing these poems was quite intense. I "moved in" with each of the Seven Words, especially the sixth one. I was very ambitious, hoping to capture some sense of "It is finished" as it has been experienced in all sorts of crucifixions since Christ's. I know that sounds arrogant, but it felt humbling and daunting, if anything.

I happened upon this obituary for Rabbi Schacter and was deeply moved by how he ran from barracks to barracks, racing against death to let the survivors know by his presence and words that they were now free. This reminded me of a story I'd read years ago by Elie Wiesel in his memoir *Night*. While in a concentration camp as a young boy, the guards made him and the other prisoners witness the hanging of a boy, then they were filed by at close range as the dying boy wiggled, his lack of weight prolonging his suffering. Someone behind Wiesel murmured, "For God's sake, where is God?" That's when Wiesel heard this voice rise up inside him: "There is where—hanging here from this gallows."

As I said earlier, I have come to see God as the Mystery of Suffering Love, the kind of living love that rises up by absorbing pain rather than inflicting it. So the depth of such love is what I was going for here, much more than any conflation of the cross and the Holocaust. But because I did not want to offend anyone inadvertently, I ran it by a rabbinical student, a Jewish poet, and a Protestant theologian. They weren't offended at all but struck by the confluence of the divine/human suffering, the never fully resolved mystery of all that. But I understand that any time you bring together Christianity and the Holocaust there's plenty of room for misunderstanding.

What do you hope people take away from these poems?

I hope they underscore that God is with and in us, even when perceived as absent, that the absence and silence of God can be a profound place of divine presence that can be trusted with our very lives.

How do you hope someone who doesn't believe in God might approach these poems?

I want to respect the integrity of my readers, but I don't usually think of them in terms of believers and non-believers. It's my experience that belief and unbelief, whether in God or humanity, wrestle in all our hearts. So my hope for those who don't believe in God is pretty much the same hope I hold for those who do believe in God: I long for these poems to foster an abiding sense of love, even amidst inexplicable suffering and loss. That's about it; the litmus test is love.

What are you working on now?

Now that I've had a few things published, I'm taking a step back and trying to see how my published works constellate. I've written much out of my childhood and youth in the Mississippi Delta of eastern Arkansas. Another cluster of poems orbits around day-to-day living and family life. Of course, there's always the God-question poems. I'm hoping to figure out the best way to sort through and arrange these as a manuscript for eventual publication.

Tell us about your writing process. Do you have a specific routine, time, or place where you write? Do you rely more on inspiration or steady work? What is revision like for you?

When I resigned from pastoring, I vowed to give myself seven years to pursue poetry. Five years later, I'm just beginning. I'm slowly learning the craft and growing by inches in my willingness to write consistently. It's essential that I begin my day in solitude and stillness, primarily through centering prayer, then try to work out of that space. My work might entail reading my way into writing, or writing my way into reading. It all depends.

Monks have a "rule," and this is mine. It's the process that I pray will become the product, a way of staying true to a very demanding calling that I'm just now venturing into, much like a child, but during the second half of life! My primary mentor is the amazing poet and teacher Matthew Lippman, though I have a small community of wonderful and patient readers who offer encouraging feedback.

How did you come to Christian faith? How did you come to poetry—was it really just five years ago? Who were your models? How did you go about learning the craft?

Being raised in the Bible Belt of eastern Arkansas, I never had much of a chance of becoming anything else. I grew up attending both Baptist and Pentecostal churches. They had me surrounded, so I surrendered! Though I was baptized as a child at nine, my faith didn't really begin to take hold in an intentional way until my college years at Arkansas State University in the 70s. That's when the love of God began to be a lived reality. My love of poetry coincided with this awakening of faith, since I then became an avid reader. I was a Philosophy major in college, but took a number of English courses. During a class in Contemporary Poetry the sky opened wide when I first read Lawrence Ferlinghetti's "Pound at Spoleto." Later, I took a Creative Writing class and tried my hand at writing poems. Though my love for poetry deepened over time, it wasn't until about ten years ago, when I was diagnosed with cancer, that prayer and poetry assumed a greater urgency. Surgery removed the cancer, but something else, a kind of fire, began to sprout up from within that my newfound health wanted to embrace. I soon began seeking out ways to devote myself more fully to the vision and craft of poetry. I took several online classes through the Gotham Writer's Workshop before entering into a mentor relationship with poet Matthew Lippman that continues to this day.

Five years ago I retired from ministry and moved both the reading and the writing of poetry closer in to the center of my calling as an exercise in faith. As a contemplative Christian, I try to embed poetry within the daily discipline of prayer/meditation/study. This means giving silence and solitude the kind of daily precedence that affords a more full-bodied listening, one that hovers about and holds together the medial region of receptive stillness and active writing/study. As I said earlier, I call this my "rule."

Since this discipline bridges the twin loves of poetry and prayer, I've never lacked for models in each of these areas, though it's rarer to find those who integrate the two. Thomas Merton continues to apprentice me in contemplation and writing. R.S. Thomas has taught me about silence, God's absence, and confirmed many of my suspicions of technocracy. Scott Cairns first opened my eyes to the call of an enfleshed holiness and the joy of discovery. Robert Penn Warren licenses my Southern voice and philosophical questioning. Gerard Manley Hopkins, especially through "The Wreck of the Deutschland" and his "dark sonnets," calls me to a kind of ascetic honesty and hope. C.D. Wright's *One with Others* draws me back to my native Delta, its heroism and demons. Philip Levine and Richard Hugo help me see my love for what's small, spare and decaying. Of course, there's always the playfulness of Hafiz and Rumi, dancing about in the background when I get too serious. As I look over my library shelves, I see too many models to mention, but many of them have taught me about the voice of faith within a Southern vernacular: Wendell Berry, Maurice Manning, Rebecca Howell, Cathy Smith-Bowers, Charles Wright, Mark Jarman, T. Crunk. So many voices and different types of spiritualities, but all resonate!

But my models are not limited to the dead or the far-away famous. I've always had close friends who love to read and have encouraged this recent turn in my journey. They've been subjected to revision after revision, often offering very helpful feedback and encouragement. For example, Belden Lane is a theologian with a poet's heart who writes prose, mostly in the area of wilderness spirituality. For years now we have met to read rough drafts over coffee or tea in the lobby of The Coronado Ballroom or at Café Ventana in midtown St. Louis. Meetings and friendships like these are my creative lifeblood.

I'm long on exuberance and short on craft. I learn best by simply trying to "write hot" and uncensored in pursuit of whatever I'm excited about or troubled by, then I revise away. I have learned craft mostly by reading what I love and asking, "What makes this work?" I seem to have a pretty good ear for things, and I try to "sound" what I'm writing for what's most authentically my own take, whatever it is we mean by "voice" and however derivative that might be. I also occasionally read books on craft. Two recent reads that I found very helpful are Mary Oliver's *A Poetry Handbook* and Stephen Dobyns' *Next Word, Better Word.* But mostly, when it comes to craft, I know I've got a lot to learn, and that's part of the excitement that keeps me at this.

Why did you give yourself seven years, and what did you think you'd do after if you didn't find yourself as a poet?

The seven years thing stems from one part Southern author Larry Brown and two parts Hebrew Scripture. I'll try to explain briefly. The biblical notion of seven as a sacred number bespeaks the Sabbath sense of restoration and wholeness. As I left pastoral ministry, I knew I had finished a pretty productive season and that it was time to let the soil of my active ministry soul lie fallow for a season. I began to give a more free rein to the introverted aspects of my life that I'd kept a tight leash on for so long. Relative to my former life, I pretty much became a hermit. About this time, I watched a documentary on author Larry Brown and was struck by how he was self-taught as a writer, that it took him about seven years of serious rejections to get published. So I latched onto seven years as an ample amount of time to try out the quest for a quiet life of contemplative writing. This has not been easy. Often I've passed through patches of restlessness and doubt: I wonder if the world really needs another poet; I question whether my fledgling ability to write rates any comparison to the knack and experience I have in pastoral ministry; I've gone whole days without times of meditation and prayer. So trying to become a prayerful poet has been a commitment I've had to renew regularly. For the most part, the "Seven-year Plan" has helped me keep my head down and ear to the ground, enough that I don't guess I've ever given serious consideration to what I'd do if I didn't find myself as a poet. Poetry and prayer have become the "non-negotiables" of my awakened heart.

What is the best advice about writing you have ever received?

"No surprise for the writer, no surprise for the reader." That comes from Robert Frost, but the poet who instilled it in me is Scott Cairns. His essay "A Troubled and Troubling Mirror," found in Emilie Griffin's *A Syllable of Water*, opened me like nothing else to poetry as discovery and to language as sacramental.

When did you start writing poetry, and what is the first poem you remember writing?

My first poem was written in college. It was about Dyess, Arkansas, my grandparents' home where I spent much of my childhood and youth. You may know it as the hometown of Johnny Cash.

What poet gives you inspiration?

Christian Wiman, if I were forced to pick just one, both for his poems and essays. I am so grateful for his definition of poetry: "Let us remember . . . that in the end we go to poetry for one reason, so that we might more fully inhabit our lives and the world in which we live them, and that if we more fully inhabit these things, we might be less apt to destroy both," from *Ambition and Survival.* I sometimes substitute "faith" for "poetry." Both work for me.

I find it interesting, though logical, that in these poems about last words, there is a drive towards wordlessness. As you say in IV: "out of words enough now/to quaff up your silence." Do you feel there is a tension between being a poet, occupied with words, and trying to get to the essence of things, to absorb the world without words getting in the way?

Your question cuts to the heart of the creative, but often frustrating, paradox of how I approach writing. I see God as other but not separate, so seeking to live out of this presence is tricky at best. We see this so well in the tension between words and silence. I seek to interweave the two pervasive strands of spirituality found at the heart of all the major religious traditions: the *apophatic*, with its *via negativa* bent, stressing the transcendence of the sacred, how God is "not this and not that"; and the *kataphatic*, with its *via positiva* affirmation of how God is revealed throughout all of life as an immanent presence. I need the *apophatic*, wordless "No" to imbue ultimacy, to purify my intentions and help me let go of my egocentric idols so that I can experience more fully the liberating effects of "not knowing." But I also need the *kataphatic*, word-filled "Yes" to affirm and manifest intimacy within the world in which I live. Without immersion in the wordlessness of silence and stillness, my loquacious ways tend toward teacup chatter, losing ultimacy; without words and actions, I am bereft of the connective power of life-giving intimacy. Both traditions are necessary, and it's within the collusion of the two that I find the "sweet spot," the promise of the paradox that is so enriching. So meditation and centering prayer have a purgative quality that helps me more fully engage the world with wonder and compassion. Or, as I noted earlier by quoting Christian Wiman, it's by virtue of silence and stillness that I am more fully able to "inhabit" the concrete and discordant world where I live.

You say in II, if you met Jesus: "I wouldn't / ask about the Father, wouldn't even / rag on Him like I used to." Could you tell us how you used to "rag on" God? How has your faith changed over the years, and do your feel that your working at the craft of poetry has deepened or altered your relationship to God?

I immediately think of something Anne Lamott once noted in her book *Bird by Bird*. How a friend once confessed, "I *could resent the ocean* if I tried." (This led Lamott to realize how much she loved that in a guy!) I spent a large part of the first half of life exploring questions of theodicy and raging about, "How can this be?" I still do, you live awhile with a faith that encourages *facing* things with your eyes open, while also trying to keep your heart half-way open, and how can you not? (I hear Jackson Browne's "Doctor My Eyes" playing in the background!) Still, at least in this particular poem, I hope to explore what it's like to be a "son," both for Jesus and myself. Poetry calls me to this kind of innocence and humility. I'm aware of all these ghosts, what the Bible refers to as "a great cloud of witnesses," that help bear me up by my deepest longing. Of course, it's this same sense of longing and "begottenness" that gives me the courage to rage against what's just not right. But I'm more interested these days in the mystery of being lifted and carried and how to honor that grace with my words and actions. Poetry helps me with all this by forcing me to get still and listen long, to pay attention to and discover anew what it is that I trust as true, however provisional my expression of that truth might be.

I guess I'm saying that I'm more interested in what it means to live with and before God and others, to explore a lived response to how God first loved/loves us all. If love is the litmus test, and I believe it is, then I'm passing through, as Johnny Cash put it, a "ring of fire" that just won't quit. It's a journey that I know most fully as a self-in -relationship that "burns, burns, burns" away my separateness, but restores my true self: I am because God is and you are, until all that is, is love.

About the Contributors

Belden C. Lane is Professor Emeritus of Theological Studies, American Religion, and History of Spirituality at Saint Louis University. He is the author of *Backpacking with the Saints: Wilderness Hiking as Spiritual Practice*, *The Solace of Fierce Landscapes: Exploring Desert and Mountain Spirituality* and *Ravished by Beauty*. He lives in St. Louis, MO, where he writes, leads retreats and provides spiritual direction.

Matthew Lippman is the author of four poetry collections: *Salami Jew* (Racing Form Press, 2014), *American Chew*, winner of The Burnside Review Book Prize (Burnside Review Book Press, 2013), *Monkey Bars* (Typecast Publishing, 2010), and *The New Year of Yellow*, winner of the Kathryn A. Morton Poetry Prize (Sarabande Books, 2007). He is the recipient of the 2014 Georgetown Review Magazine Prize and The Jerome J. Shestack Poetry Prize from *The American Poetry Review*. He teaches at Beaver Country Day School in Boston, MA.

Mud Season Review is a literary journal based in Burlington, VT that seeks to celebrate the full process of artistic creation, from inspiration to publication—welcoming into our open and collaborative community wide-ranging voices that tramp and track in the mud of human experience. The journal features monthly online (www.mudseasonreview.com) a single poet, nonfiction writer, fiction writer and artist; pairs the writing with art; and conducts interviews with its authors. Terry Minchow-Proffitt was the featured poet in Issue #3, published November 2014. He was interviewed by editor-in-chief Rebecca Starks (editor@mudseasonreview.com), and then-poetry editor Rosemary Zimmerman.

Christina Anne Taylor is the publisher at Middle Island Press and meticulously designs every poetry book with a unique signature to compliment each poet's style. She is also a poet (*Villanelle & Varia*, 2010), and a mother of three residing in West Virginia with her husband and their son.

About the Poet and Artist

Terry Minchow-Proffitt is a retired pastor who lives in St. Louis, Missouri. He was raised in the Mississippi Delta of eastern Arkansas, and continues to be inspired by his native land and its people. His poems have appeared or are forthcoming in *Arkansas Review, Big Muddy, Christian Century, decomP magazinE, Deep South Magazine, Desert Call, Freshwater, Hash, Mud Season Review, OVS Magazine, Oxford Magazine, Penwood Review, Pisgah Review, Prick of the Spindle, St. Ann's Review, Tower Journal, Valparaiso Poetry Review, Wild Violet, Words and Images Journal* and *The Write Room*.

Minchow-Proffitt received degrees in Philosophy from Arkansas State University and Theology from Princeton Theological Seminary. He has done further graduate study in English at the University of Mississippi and in Christian Spirituality at Washington Theological Union. He received certification in Spiritual Direction from The Haden Institute.

Seven Last Words is his debut collection of poems. His poem "III" was nominated for a Pushcart Prize.

To contact, he can be reached on Facebook or by email at thechickentrain@gmail.com. For more information, visit his website at Terryproffitt.jimdo.com.

Emily Mitchell is an artist, wife, mother, and art teacher, living and creating art in Vermont. For the past 20 years, she has been working as an art educator. She holds a B.A in Studio Art, Art History and Theater from Wheaton College, Massachusetts, and an M.A. Ed. in Art Education from University of Massachusetts, Dartmouth. She enjoys teaching artists of all ages, and thrives on the inspiration she receives from others.

Her approach is centered around "play," the process of letting go of what might be planned in order to honor what happens in the moment. This approach has manifested itself in varied ways throughout her creative career—in drawings, artist's books, collaborative work, and currently, paintings. When working, her heart, brain and soul are lost in the process, weaving the actual moment of painting within her response to the world. Play sets her heart singing and allows her work to ring true.

Emily has a strong visual connection to nature. As her life has grown to include her own family, her art now embraces other aspects of her sense of "home," such as mothering and parenting. Above all, she explores the human need to connect—to reach out, to feel and to understand.

Emily can be reached at emilymitchellstudio.com
or emily@emilymitchellstudio.com.

A Note on the Type

This chapbook is set in GEORGIA typeface, a transitional serif typeface designed in 1993 by Matthew Carter for the Microsoft Corporation. It was intended as a serif font that would appear elegant but legible when printed small or on low-resolution screens. The font is inspired by the Scotch Roman designs of the 19th century. Carter has successfully managed to create a typeface that combines high legibility with character and charm.

29629315R00038

Made in the USA
San Bernardino, CA
25 January 2016